Successful Plain-English IP Book For Business Leaders

Protect the Value of Your Business By Applying 15 Successful Steps to Guard Your IP

Most of the value of your business rests in your intellectual property. If you fail to take care of that property, its value will degrade.

In this carefully prepared Itty Bitty Book, Jason P. Webb shows you how to use professional IP audit techniques, written in plain English, to nurture your IP and prepare for a strong exit.

Introduce and practice these simple but important 15 processes within your company and you will protect and grow the value of your enterprise.

For example:

- Making and using simple status reports
- Finding lost or hidden money
- Marking land-mines so you avoid costly litigation

Pick up a copy of this powerful book today and experience the growth and security that come when you invest in nurturing your intellectual property.

Your Amazing
Itty Bitty®

How to Do Your
Own IP Audit

*15 Simple Steps to Keeping Your
Intellectual Property Current*

Jason P. Webb

Published by Itty Bitty Publishing
A subsidiary of S & P Productions, Inc.

This book is for informational purposes only and should not be considered legal or professional advice and does not replace the advice of an experienced attorney.

Printed in the United States of America

Itty Bitty Publishing
311 Main Street, Suite D
El Segundo, CA 90245
(310) 640-8885

ISBN: 978-1-950326-39-6

Dedication

To my friends at CEO Space

Stop by our Itty Bitty® website to find interesting information regarding **Intellectual Property.**

www.IttyBittyPublishing.com

To get a free non-disclosure agreement contact Jason at:

jasonw@pearsonbutler.com

Table of Contents

Note: Steps 1 and 2 should be done first. The rest you can do in pretty much any order and you may bounce among them.

Introduction

In this Itty Bitty Book you will find a simple process designed to be used by non-attorneys to help them keep their intellectual property (IP) healthy and current.

For most businesses with a national or international scope, IP is a critical asset. It can often be about 80% of the total value of your company. You want to take good care of it and make sure that you are not vulnerable.

Since your business changes over time, your IP assets (IP portfolio) should change, too. But, they don't automatically adjust, so you need to have a regular process to keep things current. We call that an IP Audit.

You can spend a lot of money to pay a law firm to do an audit for you, or you can manage things yourself and bring them in for their expertise when needed. More importantly, you can discover holes in your IP protection before infringers find them and that could be life or death for your company.

This Audit process is not appropriate for all businesses and does not replace working with an attorney, but it can be a good start and can save you money and protect you from trouble.

Step 1
Keeping Things EASY

IP can get complicated really quick. We want this to be easy. So let's make it easy and keep it easy:

1. Create a document entitled "Questions for my Attorney" and if you get stuck or confused on anything, add your question to the list. At the end you will go over things with your attorney and you can get them all sorted then.
2. Create a folder on your computer where you keep all your intellectual property documents and load it up. Have a separate folder in that folder for each one. There can be a lot of documents for each one and you don't want to get frustrated while trying to find things.
3. If you have patent or trademark registrations in the United States, go to www.uspto.gov and play around with the tools that they have there to find registrations and published applications. It is a great resource and you should be able to find your own registrations there. Many countries have a similar website, if you have registrations outside the US.
4. If you have copyright registrations in the US, you can find them using the tools at www.copyright.gov

Tips for organizing your files and folders

- Keep all related documents in a subfolder (e.g. all the documents filed with an application together in a folder called "Filed")
- Electronic files often come to you with names that will not make sense to you. You can rename them to things that do make sense to you.
- It is a pretty common practice for US IP attorneys to refer to registrations by the last three digits of the registration number. E.g. A patent having a registration number of 5,324,993 could be referred to as the '993 patent. It is tons easier to remember three numbers as compared to seven.
- It is also common practice for attorneys to assign a "docket number" (Docket No.) or File number ("File No.") to your files. They use that for their internal tracking. It often starts with numbers that identify the client and then ends with numbers identifying which file. If you use that same number system, it will be easier for you to coordinate correspondence and billing with your attorney.

Step 2
Getting OR Making
Your Simple Status Report

You need a big picture view of your IP – a Simple Status Report. This is a document (usually a spreadsheet) that lists out your IP assets and includes current information about them.

1. Open up a new spreadsheet document and name it IP Status Report, or something like that.
2. Put at least the following headings in a row across the sheet:
   a. Name/Title
   b. Owner
   c. Docket No.
   d. Application No.
   e. Filing Date
   f. Registration No.
   g. Registration Date
   h. Next Deadline
   i. Expected Next Costs
   j. Notes
3. Name each piece of IP you have down the Name/Title column and fill out as much of the rest as you can. If you can't fill something out, don't worry, that will be addressed that later.

Tips for knowing what IP to list on the Simple Status Report

- Every patent, trademark, and copyright that you have registered, separately listed for every registration in every country where you have it registered
- Every patent, trademark, and copyright application that you have filed but is not yet registered, separately listed for every registration in every country where you have it filed
- Every patent, trademark, and copyright that you have not filed yet, but plan to file, separately listed for every registration in every country where you have planned to file
- Each trade secret that you want to specifically track (e.g. product formulation, preferred vendor list, manufacturing process steps)
- Important contracts/agreements (e.g. client agreement, vendor agreement, supplier agreement)
- Anything that you think needs to be protected, but you are not sure how yet
- Important website/URL ownership
- User accounts (e.g. social media)

Step 3
Keeping Things ALIVE

One of the biggest risks in IP is losing registrations/applications because they expire or abandon due to a failure to do the right thing at the right time. Part of the problem is that some of the deadlines are years away.

1. Make sure that your simple status report has an entry for each application and each registration in the Next Deadline column, even if it is an NA (for not applicable, where there is no current deadline).
2. Update your simple status report during the year as new deadlines come and go.
3. Calendar these deadlines in whatever calendaring system you use to keep track of your life and include reminders in anticipation of these deadlines.
4. Calendar tasks for yourself sufficient to make sure that you will have the money and other resources needed on time to meet the deadline.
5. Sometimes deadlines are extendable and some are not. Plan on them not being extendable.
6. If not sure that missing a deadline will be fatal to the IP, assume it is.

Some examples of deadlines that can end rights if missed

- Priority deadlines (e.g. the one year deadline to claim priority to a provisional application, deadline to file foreign applications that claim the benefit of a US application).
- Office Action deadlines (i.e. the deadline to respond to a rejection of an application).
- Deadline to file a patent application due to a public disclosure for an invention (generally 1 year from the date of disclosure in the US, but zero days for pretty much every other country)
- Renewals and Maintenance Filings
- Trademark statement of use/extension deadlines
- Annuity filings (an annual fee required to be paid on an application that is required by most countries outside the US)
- Notices of incomplete filings
- Notices of incorrect responses/filings
- Decisions on Appeal

Step 4
Herding

Here is where you deal with missing and incomplete information. Imagine that your Status Report is a nice safe fenced-in area for your IP. Now, herd them all in.

1. Highlight cells on your spreadsheet where you are missing information or need help.
2. Put notes in the highlighted cells about what you have done or what you are doing to resolve the missing information.
3. Send emails and/or make phone calls as necessary to get missing information.
4. Schedule reminders in your calendar, as appropriate, to remind you to follow up on the highlighted cells, individually or as a set.
5. Schedule times to make more definite plans for IP that is just in the planning stage and needs to move forward (e.g. a customer agreement that has not been written or updated yet).

Common issues that "herding" helps solve

- Missing filing/registration information for an application/registration
- Office Action received, but no clear plan has been developed for the response
- Office Action received, there is a plan, but the response requires research or evidence that has not been gathered yet
- "I thought we filed that application"
- Rushing to get money for a deadline
- Feeling overwhelmed

Tips for effective "herding"

- If you need several things from someone, you can send each one in a separate email. They are more likely to respond quicker and less likely to save it for "when I have time to get to all this."
- Highlight with different colors for different things. E.g. yellow = I need to research that, blue = waiting for details from someone else.
- When you schedule planning time for yourself, paste relevant details (including instructions to yourself) into the appointment so that you don't have to hunt for it at the time.
- Don't get stuck on this step, keep going, even if you have highlighted cells.

Step 5
Spotting Vulnerabilities

Your Simple Status report is now a map you can use to spot vulnerabilities in your IP portfolio. Go through the following, there is a potential vulnerability in each one.

1. Go over any cells that are still highlighted.
2. Pay special attention to planned applications/contracts that are not yet filed or drafted.
3. Pay special attention to the ownership column. IP grants monopoly rights, but if there are different owners for the different parts of your portfolio, the monopoly is fractured/weakened.
4. Compare what is protected with the realities of your business and make notes of where they don't seem to match
5. Check your gut feeling about things that are incomplete or in process and decide if you should explore augmenting those properties with extra protection.

Some Common Vulnerabilities

- Your registered trademarks don't match up exactly with how you are using them in your marketing/advertising
- Your customers have a nickname for your business/product and you don't have a trademark registration for it
- You are far along in product/system development for something new for your business and have not talked with your attorney yet, researched potential infringement, or made plans for protection
- You have a successful product/service but no registered IP
- The business partners own the IP separately instead of the company owning it or a holding company owning it
- You have an important IP application that the government keeps rejecting (more than once with trademark/copyright or more than 3-4 times with patent)
- Someone (e.g. business partner, competitor, strategic alliance partner, customer) is using your IP without formal written permission

Step 6
Finding Money

Your Simple Status Report can also be a map to find money. Let's take a look and see what we can find:

1. Look for registrations that don't match up with the realities of your business. Maybe you don't need to spend money to keep them alive anymore.
2. Look at what you own and think about who is using your IP and not paying for it.
3. Look at who you are selling/licensing your IP to and think about who else might want it.
4. Look at who is supposed to be paying you money (e.g. licensing) and double check to make sure that they actually are.

Some examples of "found money"

- Trademark and patent registrations that no longer cover anything commercially relevant – stop paying to keep the dead weight alive.
- Licensees who have not been paying royalties.
- Patents/trademarks/copyrights that can be licensed into new non-competing verticals (e.g. industrial tech that could be made into a toy/novelty item).
- Consolidated filings (e.g. saving money on applications because you negotiate a bulk discount, filing multi-class trademark applications).

Step 7
Predicting The Future
By Creating The Future

You want to be in a great position in the future when it comes time to exit your business. Don't leave that to chance:

1. Imagine/research/plan what your exit might look like (e.g. bought out by a larger company, public stock offering, sale to your heirs).
2. Think about and research what the next owner will want to own and why they want to own that.
3. Think about what your Simple Status Report will look like when that happens. This is your Desired Status Report.
4. Think about how you will use the Desired Status Report to show great value in the business. You might even create a faux report to help clarify what that would look like.
5. Go back to your actual Simple Status Report and add whatever planned IP needs to be added and change whatever instructions/notes need to be changed to head you in the direction of your Desired Status Report.

Food for thought when planning/creating a future

- Maybe your exit does not hand over all the IP or all to one new owner.
- Since things rarely go exactly as planned, maybe have more than one exit plan.
- If you don't think you need an exit plan, remember that everyone leaves their job, at least when they die, and that is an exit, too.
- The faux report can really help you have a clear vision for the future, writing/typing things out activates more parts of your brain
- It is hard to guess what a prospective purchaser wants to buy from you – but you can do research on them and find out what they value.
- Your Simple Status Report is a working document, not an end product or result
- Your IP is tied, directly or indirectly, to all aspects of your business, and vice-versa.

Step 8
Checking The Fences

There are some especially vulnerable "locations" where your IP can leak out. Perhaps the most common leak is through relationships, i.e. your neighbors (e.g. employees, customers, suppliers, contractors). Use your Simple Status Report to check the fences with your neighbors:

1. Make a list of all of the most important relationships or relationship types in your business.
2. Compare that list to the list of agreements/contracts that show up on your Simple Status report.
3. Add plans for agreements that are missing.
4. Check the agreements that you do have for important terms.
5. Think about problems that you have had with those relationships or other similar ones.
6. Make notes of any terms that you think should be there but are missing.
7. Schedule time to fix the fences.

Some common clauses in agreements that help make good fences

- Confidentiality (aka Non-Disclosure or
- Safekeeping and Return of Confidential Materials).
- NDA
- Licensing
- Assignment of Rights
- Termination
- Non-compete
- Non-solicitation of employees
- Non-solicitation of customers
- Royalty payment terms
- Work for hire
- Ownership
- Liquidated damages
- Right to Injunction
- Indemnification
- Relationship (e.g. not partners, not agents)
- Warrantees

Step 9
Traveling Through Time

Your IP protection generally protects your IP as it was you who instituted the protection. It doesn't automatically change as time passes. In some ways you have to manually "travel through time" in order to keep it current.

1. Check your copyright notices on assets that are continually published (e.g. on your website) and update them to the current year. E.g. I changed © JP Webb 2012 – 2017 to © JP Webb 2012 – 2018 in my January 2018 audit.
2. Check your trademark notices and make sure that you have TM on the ones where you are using branding but don't have a registration and using ® on the ones where you are using branding and DO have a trademark registration.
3. Check your patent notices to make sure that you have Pat. Pend. notices where you have a patent application pending that covers the product/service, that you have Patent No. ### (with the actual number) where you have an associated patent registration, and that you have removed those notices where they are no longer valid.

More ways to "travel through time"

- Branding experts often recommend that you modernize your logo every 5 – 10 years. File new trademark application(s) to cover changes to your branding (e.g. a modernized logo)
- Buy more domains that are related to your branding and point them at your website(s).
- Review your contracts, especially customer agreements, and make sure that they match up with how you are actually doing business today.
- Double-check how you are protecting your trade secrets and update any processes that seem weak or leaky.

Step 10
Swallowing Frogs

You've now had time to get some of your highlighted cells sorted out. There are probably some that you've been putting off, i.e. frogs that you don't want to swallow. Let's take care of those.

1. Look through the highlighted cells and find any that haven't been done but may get done if you delegate them to someone else. Do that.
2. Look through the highlighted cells and find any that you really need an attorney to help with. Call/email your attorney and get that help.
3. Look through the highlighted cells and predict if you will really get it resolved before your next audit. If you think not, then change it to a color that means "not this time."
4. Schedule a time to repeat this, maybe in a month and scheduled as the first thing you do that day.

Research resources

Sometimes you put things off because you don't understand them. If you are putting something off, then do research to better understand that subject matter. You may find yourself more able and willing to do it. Here are some research resources that have good IP materials:

- www.uspto.gov
- www.copyright.gov
- www.en.wikipedia.org/wiki/Patent
- www.en.wikipedia.org/wiki/Trademark
- www.en.wikipedia.org/wiki/Copyright
- www.en.wikipedia.org/wiki/Trademark_Dilution
- www.en.wikipedia.org/wiki/Trade_Secret
- www.en.wikipedia.org/wiki/Assignment_(law)
- www.wipo.int/about-ip/en/
- www.patentlyo.com
- www.ipwatchdog.com
- www.stopfakes.gov

Step 11
Learning From The Past

If you don't learn from the past you are doomed to repeat it, right?

1. Look back on the year and make a list of experiences with your customers, employees, partners, vendors, supplier, etc. that you do not want to repeat.
2. Mark each experience that could have been avoided by a term in a contract.
3. Mark each experience that could have been avoided by better educational materials in your process.
4. Mark each experience that could have been avoided with some technology that you have thought of.
5. Go through your marks and decide what would be the best way (e.g. most efficient, most cost effective, most effective) to avoid those kinds of experiences in the future.
6. Schedule times to start implementation of each way that you want to go forward with.

Some ideas for avoiding problems

- Bold/highlight/underline/etc. terms in your contracts that people seem to miss.
- Create a customer welcome program that teaches your customers what to expect and how to best get value from your goods/services.
- Include leaflets, guides, etc. in your product packaging that guide your customers to avoid common problems.
- Create educational materials for people that you interact with that teach them how to avoid problems (e.g. video series for new employees, FAQ for customers).
- Call your business attorney to see how they might change your agreements to prevent some of the problems that you have had.
- Review your competitors materials to see how they might be solving those same problems
- Think about what might be better/different if you changed the order of steps in your processes

Step 12
Marking Land-Mines

Now that you have a pretty good idea of what you own and are taking steps to improve your IP portfolio, you probably also have ideas for how you want to grow your business. You want to do this safely, so mark some land mines:

1. Any changes or additions to your branding should be researched to explore whether you might be infringing someone else's rights. Have your IP attorney do a basic trademark screening search.
2. If you have a product that has a production quality prototype you can have a freedom to operate search done to help make sure that you are not infringing someone else's patent.
3. Review any cease and desist notices and related notes and check to make sure that you are not accidentally overstepping into areas where you have decided to avoid. You can also review any competitors to see if they are infringing your materials.

Some common IP dangers

- Infringing trademark rights, especially when entering a new market, country, or launching a new product/service.
- Infringing patent rights, especially when entering a new market, country, or launching a new product/service.
- Infringing copyright rights, especially when hiring third parties to create materials for you (e.g. web developer who steals images off the internet to use in building your website).
- Acting like you own copyright rights in art, photographs, etc. that you paid for someone else to create for your business without having a written agreement saying that you own it.
- Copying a competitor's product/packaging without doing formal legal research.
- Using branding that is similar to famous brands or brands owned by very large companies as they tend to very aggressively protect their trademarks.

Step 13
Protecting The Defenseless

Look at your Simple Status Report. If there are any items of intellectual property or planned property that don't have sufficient protection, now is the time to get that going.

1. File trademark, patent, and copyright applications where appropriate.
2. Draft contracts, where appropriate.
3. Send cease-and-desist letters, where appropriate
4. Add notices to your marketing and advertising materials, including product packaging, where appropriate
5. You might not have sufficient funds to do everything now that needs to be done, but you can get quotes and prioritize getting that protection.

Sample costs to prepare and file various types of IP protection

- Federal Trademark application in the US: $600 - $2500
- Utility Patent Application in the US: $6500 - $12,000
- Copyright Application in the US: $400 - $900
- Trade secret protection: free (no registration to file), but generally imposes process costs due to reasonable steps required to keep it secret
- Customs and Border registration $300 - $900
- Design patent application in the US: $1500 - $2500

Step 14
Handling Expiration Dates

IP rights expire after a time. Sometimes you can renew them, sometimes not. An expiration date may be on your Simple Status Report.

1. For trademark expiration dates, they can be renewed, indefinitely, as long as you are still using the brand in commerce. Be sure that you are still using the brand in commerce and coordinate with your attorney to have it renewed.

2. For copyright expiration dates, you can create updated versions of what is protected and file a new copyright application on that newer material. Be sure to include things in the newer material that will make it worth buying instead of buying the old stuff. That said, copyright registrations last a very long time, so unless you are in the 3rd or 4th generation of a business, you probably will not face this issue.

3. For patent expiration dates (assuming that you have handled all the maintenance filings), you have to make a patentable improvement to the technology and file a new application. You can't just file the same patent over again and expect it to give you rights.

Some ideas for creating new materials/ inventions

- Think about how new advances in technology can be implemented in your materials/inventions. E.g. when great improvements in LED lights occurred, many people found new uses for them in thousands of products.
- Think about how recent changes in culture apply to your materials/inventions. Culture changes often include changes in values that change how people view/use products and services.
- Take a class in something that is very different from what you already know, this can get your creative juices flowing.
- Think about your materials/inventions while you exercise.
- Sign up to be your own customer and take notes about the experience.
- Make a list of ten impossible improvements to your materials/inventions that people would LOVE to buy from you and start making plans on how you could actually deliver them, this can spark possible improvements.

Step 15
Coordinating With Your Attorney

You've been working with a Simple Status Report and have used it to improve your IP portfolio and to come up with more ideas on how you can make it even better. You are now in a great position to leverage your IP attorney's knowledge and experience to get maximum value out of that relationship.

1. Schedule a correlation meeting with your IP attorney and get clarity as to what the billing for that meeting will be.
2. Share your Simple Status Report with your IP attorney.
3. Share your Desired Status Report with your IP attorney.
4. Talk through your exit plans with your IP attorney.
5. Get advice on the feasibility of your plans and how you plan to secure the rights you need to execute your exit plans.
6. Get quotes for filings/registrations.
7. Have your IP attorney confirm that your report matches theirs.

Some questions you might want to ask your IP attorney

- Will you take a quick look at my website/packaging and let me know if you see anything that looks off?
- How else can I protect my business?
- Do you know anybody that might be a good networking contact for me? (attorneys tend to be well connected)
- Do you know anybody who does [whatever skill-set you are looking for]?
- Are there other exit strategies that I might not be considering?
- If you were me, what would you change in my IP strategy?
- How can we do more business together at a high value to my business?
- Are there other attorneys that you know and trust that you think I should meet?

You've finished. Before you go...

Tweet/share that you finished this book.

Please star rate this book.

Reviews are solid gold to writers. Please take a few minutes to give us some itty bitty feedback.

ABOUT THE AUTHOR

Jason is married with five kids and there are more computers in his home than there are people. His power bill always shows him as #1 compared to his neighbors and someday he expects to receive an award of some sort for that.

He's always been a voracious reader of non-fiction and science-fiction/fantasy. He once wrote a software mod for the game Skyrim and he still plays Dungeons and Dragons with old friends.

Jason is a big fan of non-violent communication, especially in the family. Jason secretly hopes for a zombie apocalypse, because that would be so cool. No, that would be terrible. (So cool!!)

If you enjoyed this Amazing Itty Bitty® Book
you might also benefit from:

- **Your Amazing Itty Bitty® Little Black Book of Sales** – Anthony Camacho

- **Your Amazing Itty Bitty® Prospects-to-Profits Lead Generation Book** – Erin Smilkstein

- **Your Amazing Itty Bitty® Guide to being TED Worthy** – John-Alfred Kohler Bates

Or any of the many other Amazing Itty Bity®
Books available online at
www.ittybittypublishing.com